This book belongs to

amiepotter

STORY COLLECTION
Jungle

Written by Ronne Randall
Illustrated by Jacqueline East
Design by The Dirty Cat Company.

This is a Parragon book
This edition published in 2004

Parragon,
Queen Street House
4 Queen Street
Bath
BA1 1HE, UK

Printed in China

ISBN 1-40543-983-1

Contents

Snap Happy...................6

Hippo's Holiday.............12

Monkey Mayhem...........18

Snap Happy

One lazy morning, Claudia Crocodile was drifting down the river, looking for fun.

Up ahead, she could see Mickey and Maxine Monkey and Chico Chimp playing on the riverbank. "I think I'll give them a fright," decided Claudia. "It's always amusing to watch them run away!"

Flashing and gnashing her sharp teeth, she swam towards the three friends. Sure enough, the SNAP! SNAP! SNAP! of Claudia's jaws scared the little monkeys.

"RUN," cried Maxine, "before she snaps our tails off!"

They tumbled over each other as they climbed to safety.

"Hee, hee!" Claudia laughed as she watched them. "Scaring the monkeys is such fun!"

That afternoon, Claudia was bored again, so she looked for someone else to frighten. "Aha!" she said.

"There's little Timmy Tiger, paddling all by himself. I'll give him a real fright!" And she set off down the river, SNAP-SNAP-SNAPPING as she went.

Timmy didn't hear Claudia, until she was right behind him! SNAP! SNAP! went her great big jaws. GNASH! GNASH! GNASH! went her sharp, pointy teeth. "AAAAGGGGGHHH!" screamed Timmy, as he saw Claudia's mouth open wide. He tried to run away, but his paws were stuck in the mud! Claudia came closer and closer. Timmy trembled with terror.

"You're supposed to run away!" Claudia whispered.

"I c-c-can't," stammered Timmy. "I'm stuck!"

"Oh," said Claudia, disappointed. "It's no fun if you don't run away.""Aren't you g-going to eat me?" gulped Timmy. "EAT YOU?" roared Claudia. "Yuck! You're all furry! I prefer fish."

"Really?" said Timmy. "Then why are you always snapping and gnashing and frightening everyone?"

"Because that's what crocodiles do!" said Claudia. "We're supposed to be scary. Er… you won't tell anyone I didn't eat you, will you?" she asked, helping Timmy climb out of the mud. "Don't worry," laughed Timmy, "I won't tell!"

"Thanks for un-sticking me," Timmy said. "I never knew you could be nice. I like you!"

Claudia's green face blushed bright red!

"I think everyone would like you," went on Timmy, "if you just tried to be friendly, instead of scary."

"Oh, I don't think I can do that," said Claudia. "My jaws simply HAVE to snap and my teeth just MUST gnash! I can't help it."

"Wait!" said Timmy. "I know just how you can be friendly and helpful and snap and gnash at the same time! Here's your chance."

As Timmy and Claudia went along together, they saw Mickey and Maxine trying to smash open some coconuts. Claudia swam towards the monkeys, SNAP-SNAP-SNAPPING with her jaws. As soon as they heard her, the monkeys ran for the nearest tree.

"I just want to help," said Claudia, climbing on to the bank. "Throw me a coconut!" And with a SNAP! SNAP! SNAP! quick as a flash, Mickey's coconut was open. Then Claudia opened Maxine's coconut, too and soon everyone was sharing the cool, refreshing milk and chewy chunks of coconut. Claudia had never shared anything and found that she liked it!

Chico Chimp came running towards his friends. He was carrying a big watermelon. Suddenly, Chico spotted Claudia, whose jaw was open, ready to SNAP! "Uh-oh!" he gulped, turning to run.

"Don't worry, Chico," said Maxine. "Throw Claudia the watermelon!" Chico watched in amazement as Claudia SNAP-SNAP-SNAPPED the watermelon into neat slices for everyone. "Thanks, Claudia!" they all chorused. Chico gave Claudia the biggest slice. Then Emma, Eric and Ellen Elephant came trundling down to the river with bundles of thick branches in their trunks. "We're going to make a raft!" said Emma – and then they saw Claudia.

As the frightened elephants galloped away, Claudia picked up the branches they had dropped. SNAP! SNAP! GNASH! GNASH! went Claudia's strong jaws and sharp teeth. "Wow! Thanks, Claudia!" said Emma, as the elephants came back. "That was really helpful!"

Claudia grinned. Being friendly and helpful was rather nice! "Here we go!" shouted the elephants, when their raft was ready.

The friends on the riverbank watched them.

"That looks like so much fun!" said Chico. "Can you help us make a raft, too, Claudia?"

"I can do even better," said Claudia. "Hop on my back!"

"WHEEE! This is GREAT!" whooped Maxine as they sailed down the river on Claudia's back.

Happiest of all was Claudia, who had found that having friends was much more fun than scaring them!

Hippo's Holiday

It was a warm, sunny morning in the jungle. "A perfect time for a long, relaxing wallow," thought Howard Hippo. Wallowing in the river was Howard's favourite thing to do. He found a nice, cool, muddy spot and settled in. Howard was just drifting off into a delightful daydream, when... SPLASH! "Gotcha!" shrieked Maxine Monkey. SPLOOSH! "Gotcha back!" shouted Chico Chimp.

"Can't you monkeys and chimps play somewhere else?" Howard grumbled. "I'm wallowing here!"

"Oops! Sorry, Howard," Maxine apologised. But it was too late. Howard's wallow was ruined. That afternoon, as the hot sun beat down on his back, Howard slithered into the river to cool off.

"Aaah," he breathed, as he soaked in the cool water. "This is sooo lovely."

"Yoo-hoo! Howard!" called Penelope Parrot. "I've just learned to do a double-rollover-loop-the-loop! Want to see?" "Sure, Penelope," sighed Howard. It didn't look as if he was going to have a chance to relax this afternoon, either! The next morning, Howard's cousin, Hilary, came to visit. "You look exhausted, Howard," she said.

"That's because I never have a chance to relax and wallow any more," said Howard.

"What you need is a holiday," said Hilary. "I'm leaving for Hippo Hollow this afternoon. Why don't you come with me?" "That sounds like a good idea!" said Howard. "You'll love Hippo Hollow," said Hilary, as the two hippos trundled through the jungle.

"There's so much mud!"

Howard saw himself relaxing in a cool mud bath.

"And there are streams and waterfalls!"continued
Hilary. Howard imagined having lots of cool showers.

"And everyone has lots and lots of FUN!" finished
Hilary. Howard thought about playing games with new
hippo friends.

At last Howard and Hilary arrived at Hippo Hollow.
"It's even more beautiful than
I had imagined!" Howard exclaimed. "And it looks like
we've arrived just in time!" said Hilary.

"For what?" asked Howard. "A relaxing mud bath?"
"No, silly!" laughed Hilary. "Hippo-robics!"

"Let's get moving, everyone!" called a sleek-looking
hippo. Lots of other hippos galloped into the stream
behind her.

"Come on, Howard," said Hilary. "Don't be a party
pooper on the first day of your holiday!"

Howard had no choice but to join in. "Kick, two,
three, four! Kick, two, three, four!" shouted the
instructor.

Howard did his best and kicked with all the others.
"Surely everyone will want a nice, long rest after all this

exercise?" he thought. But he was wrong! After a quick
shower in the waterfall, everyone rushed off to play
Volley-Melon and Hilary wanted Howard on her team.
Howard finally did get to have a rest after lunch – but
not for long! "You're looking much more relaxed,
Howard," Hilary called, as she led her junior swimming
class right past him. "This holiday was just what you
needed, wasn't it?"

"Er… I guess so,"
Howard replied, weakly.

After his busy day, Howard was hoping for an early night.He was just getting settled, when he heard Hilary.

"Come on, Howard!" she bellowed. "You don't want to miss the Hippo-Hooray Cabaret! They are really good!"

"Oh – YAWN – how wonderful," sighed Howard. He could barely keep his eyes open.

The next morning, Howard was sliding into the river, when he heard Hilary calling.

"Is it time for Hippo-robics?" he asked.

"Oh, no," said Hilary. "Lots of good, fresh air is what you need. So we're going on a hike!" Howard huffed and puffed all through the exhausting hike. "I hope I can have a nice cool bath when this is over,"
he thought. Howard got his wish. But, as he was soaking his sore muscles, Hilary came by for a chat.

"The hike was fun, wasn't it?" she said.

"Oh yes," said Howard. "In fact, I enjoyed it so much, that I've decided to go on another one!"

"Really?" said Hilary. "That's great!
Where are you hiking to?"

"Home!" said Howard. "I'm going home, where I can have a REAL holiday. And where there are no Hippo-robics, and no Volley-Melon games, no cabarets and no one to stop me wallowing as long as I like!"

And so that's exactly what Howard did!

Monkey Mayhem

Mickey and Maxine Monkey had finished their breakfast of Mango Munch. Now they were rushing off to play. "Be careful!" called their mum. "And please DON'T make too much noise!"

"We won't!" the two mischievous monkeys promised, leaping across to the next tree. "Wheeee," screeched Mickey, and "Wa-hoooo!" hollered Maxine. The noise echoed through the whole jungle – Mickey and Maxine just didn't know how to be quiet! Ka-thunk! Mickey landed on a branch. Ka-clunk! Maxine landed beside him. Ker-aack! "Ooohh noooo!" the monkeys hollered as the branch snapped. "Yi-i-i-kes!" they shrieked, as they went tumbling down. Ker-thumpp! The jungle shook as the two monkeys crashed to the ground.

"Yipppeeee!" the monkeys cheered, jumping up happily. "That was so much FUN!" exclaimed Maxine.

18

"Let's go and get Chico Chimp and see if he wants to do it, too!" And the two monkeys scrambled back up to the tree tops, bellowing, "HEY, CHICO! COME AND PLAY WITH US!" as they swung through the branches.

All over the jungle, animals shook their heads and covered their ears. Couldn't anyone keep those naughty, noisy monkeys quiet? Chico Chimp arrived to play with his friends. The three of them were having a great time swinging, tumbling and bouncing together when suddenly they stopped short. Grandpa Gorilla was standing in their path, glaring at them angrily.

"Go away, you mischief-makers," he said. "You've given us all enough headaches today.

My grandson Gulliver is fast asleep by the river and, if you wake him up, I will be very, very upset!"

"Sorry," whispered Maxine, looking down at the ground. Everyone in the jungle knew it was a big mistake to upset Grandpa Gorilla!

"We'll be quiet," they promised.

Mickey, Maxine and Chico didn't know what to do until Mickey said, "Let's climb the coconut palm tree. We can do that quietly."

"Okay," the others agreed half-heartedly.

"I suppose it's better than doing nothing," said Maxine. From their perch among the coconuts, the three friends could see right over the jungle. They saw Jerome Giraffe showing his son Jeremy how to choose the juiciest, most tender leaves on a tree… and they saw Portia Parrot giving her daughter Penelope her first flying lesson. And right down below them, they saw little Gulliver Gorilla sleeping contentedly in the tall grass beside the river.

And – uh-oh! They saw something else, too… Claudia Crocodile was in the river. She was grinning and snapping her big, sharp teeth – and heading straight for

Gulliver! The friends didn't think twice. Maxine shouted, "GET UP, GULLIVER! GET UP RIGHT NOOOOOOWW!"

Then Mickey and Chico began throwing coconuts at Claudia.

SMAACCCK! they went, on Claudia's hard crocodile head.

"OWW-WOOW!" moaned Claudia.

"What's going on here?" Grandpa Gorilla shouted up into the coconut tree. "I thought I told you three to keep quiet!"

All the noise woke Gulliver. The little gorilla sat up, looked around, and ran to his grandpa, who was hurrying towards the river. When Grandpa saw Claudia he realised what had happened. "I am so glad you're safe!" he said, giving Gulliver a great big gorilla hug. The three monkeys came down from the tree.

"We're sorry we made so much noise," Chico said.

By this time all the gorillas had gathered around, and so had most of the other animals.

"What's going on?" squawked Portia Parrot.

"Yes, what's all the commotion about?" asked Jerome Giraffe.

"These three youngsters are heroes," said Grandpa. "They have saved my grandson from being eaten by Claudia Crocodile!"

"I think you all deserve a reward," said Grandpa. "And I think it should be…"

"Hurrah!" cheered all the other animals and then they held their breath in anticipation.

"…permission to be just as noisy as you like, whenever you like!" Grandpa Gorilla announced.

"YIPPEEE!" cheered Mickey, Maxine and Chico, in their loudest, screechiest voices. Their grins were almost as wide as the river.

"OH, NOOOOO!" all the other animals groaned together – but they were all smiling, too.